How to Quit Drugs

STANLEY ARTHUR

ISBN-13: 978-1544635712

ISBN-10: 1544635710

DEDICATION

This book is dedicated to the still-suffering addict.

May you find your way to the support you need to get and stay clean.

To your family, may they find the strength to love you and support
you through this tough transition.

To all of those people inside and outside of the rooms who dedicate
their lives to staying clean and helping others get and stay clean.

To my friends and family who put up with all my shit over the years
and to the ones I had to leave behind.

I hope you find what you need.

Peace. Love. Unity. Respect.

CONGRATULATIONS

You made it!

You no longer have to use drugs.

You no longer have to die.

You are now part of this amazing worldwide community of

recovering addicts.

No matter where you end up in this world, you will have support.

You no longer have to die from this disease and better yet, you can

now go on to live a long and happy life filled with love, joy and

excitement.

It will not always be easy, but you really can get through it.

I believe in you.

We believe in you.

CONTENTS

ACKNOWLEDGMENTS

I would like to acknowledge the people and principles which help people around the world get and stay clean. Each person is individual but with the help of one another, we are able to combat our addiction and arrest it where it stands. This book is not meant to speak for or represent any of the 12-step fellowships but more just show sheer gratitude for the freedom and life that I have been given to carry my message to the still suffering addict. It is only with the help of a loving god and worldwide family that I have been gifted with the ability to do so. As we can only keep what we have by giving it away, so please take what I have to give so that I can live another day.

PREFACE

Addiction is a cunning enemy of life.

I cannot say you will no longer be an addict after reading this. I can however give you a few of the most useful tools and suggestions, which have helped me, quit drugs once and for all. At very least, it will help get you through the initial phases of quitting drugs and hopefully shine some light on ways that will help you stay off of drugs for good. I have learned these lessons from spending 13 years of my life in active addiction and then the last 1000 days learning how to move on and create a better life for myself and for those around me. I hope it can help you do the same. Truly embrace the following suggestions. Open your mind to truly accept them and take action right away.

CHAPTER 1

ADMIT YOU HAVE A PROBLEM

Deep down you know you have a problem.

Say it out loud right now.

Do it.

Say it after me.

I have a problem.

"I have a problem."

There you did it!

Good job!

Now, you need to figure out what the problem is and how to

fix it.

If you think that your problem is drugs or alcohol that is great.

We have something to work with.

Addiction in itself seems to manifest in so many different ways throughout the process of "getting clean," but that does not mean that we cannot overcome it.

A lot of time, it can move into things like eating, coffee, relationships, isolation, depression, etc.

Through listening to the suggestions in this book however, we will get through it and you will be able to live a happy life once again.

So, lets get started.

CHAPTER 2

MAKE THE DECISION TO QUIT DRUGS

Wouldn't it be nice, if this were the only thing you needed to do? If it was this easy, drugs wouldn't be nearly the problem for our loved ones and so many people would not be dying on our streets every day.

It would be awesome if we could just decide to quit drugs and simply stick to it.

If that were the case, I wouldn't need to write this book.

Also, I would have been clean and sober years before overdosing and losing many of my good friends to this horrific disease.

I am sure there would be a lot more clean and sober people around as well.

At the end of every weekend, many of your friends would probably clean up and go on to become productive and respectable members of society.

Unfortunately that is not what happens.

At the end of each weekend or each bender, many of us get that feeling in our gut where we know we need to stop.

We feel the pain, depression and anxiety within ourselves and maybe even recognize how we are hurting the ones around us.

We have had enough of this repetitive life as a drug addict and don't want to do it any more.

Sometimes, we are even able to string together a few days or weeks

clean and think that we are good now.

If you go a week or two, you begin to think that maybe you don't

even have a problem.

You have a job right?

Or you pay your bills so why can't you go party now and again?

The truth is that maybe some people can go out for a drink or recreationally dip into drugs now and again and be fine.

Maybe they can just go out for an hour or two, have some drinks and then go home to bed without wanting to keep the party going.

I know absolutely fucking nothing about this type of person.

What I do know is that if this decision is ever going to stick, you need to be absolutely 100% committed to this decision.

You admitted you have a problem so you make the decision to get clean.

I have learned time and time again that if you are kind of on the fence or unsure about this decision, you will fail 100% of the time.

You need to actually decide and commit to that decision that you will not do drugs any more.

You need to make the decision yourself.

You cannot make the decision for someone else to quit and nobody can make the decision for you.

You can try, but it will not work.

You can guide somebody to make the decision, but each of us need to decide that we will quit or it will never stick.

CHAPTER 3

MAKE A PLAN

Once you make the decision, you need come up with a plan.

This will consist of what actions you will do to help your decision stick.

Your plan does not have to be all encompassing or even written down but that definitely does help.

Even if your plan was just to buy this book or reach out for help, as long as you have some sort of action planned, your chances on sticking to it increase dramatically.

I mentioned writing it down.

This is a great strategy.

Nothing helps goals get accomplished better than writing them down.

Put it somewhere that you will look at it, maybe on your wall or in a journal.

Writing down your plan when it comes to quitting drugs and continuously returning to this document to hold yourself accountable will definitely help.

You definitely do not have to write down your plan.

Your plan could simply be to make a phone call.

Ask someone for help or admit that you have a problem.

When I hit my rock bottom, I was in midst of a 10-day bender where I overdosed, kept doing drugs, got depressed, was trying to kill myself and by the grace of god survived.

Only then, was I finally able to reach out.

You do not have to wait that long.

I need to stress that.

A lot of addicts I meet, give up because they think that their problem isn't that bad or because other people's situations are much worse.

It's true that there will always people who were in much worse

situations when they first decided to get clean.

I can tell you one thing for sure.

You are here for a reason.

You would not be reading this book unless you really want to quit

drugs and finally end this depressing lifestyle.

The same goes if you are looking at this book for somebody else.

You are looking at this for a reason.

You suspect someone might have a problem.

I guarantee that you are right.

You wouldn't be looking otherwise.

CHAPTER 4

STRATEGIZE

Come up with a strategy for your plan.

Like I said, it will not always be easy.

Have some proven strategies ready for when times get tough.

Have a list of ways that you will deal with life, at least in the short term, to ensure you can successfully handle any issue that comes your way.

This section of your plan will be developed and modified in time when you realize what is needed and what works for you.

I can however give you some tips which have worked quite well for myself and if they sound like they could help you, write them down as part of your plan and refer back to it whenever you are having an issue or you are wanting to go party or use drugs.

You can even write them in this book.

I left you lots of space to jot down notes and feelings should you feel the need.

So go ahead.

Express yourself.

CHAPTER 5

CONTACT SUPPORTS

For me, starting out this first meant calling a certain couple of coworkers and letting them know I needed help.

Then once I learned about meetings, it was going to a meeting.

At the meetings, I met people and it was suggested to me to take a meeting list of guys with phone numbers who agreed to be supports.

Your number one thing when you are struggling should be to contact your supports, whether it's a meeting, someone you met, a family member, close (sober) friend or even your pet cat, get in touch with someone who will calm you down off that ledge.

I know first hand that sometimes, the phone can be the heaviest

thing in the world when you need to call someone for support.

Nobody likes to feel vulnerable and it is understandable that

sometimes you find it difficult to reach out.

Or maybe you do find the strength to pick up the phone and call

someone.

Or you were too scared so you texted.

Unfortunately the people you do reach out to may be unreachable at

that time.

Don't take it as a personal attack like I did at the start.

Other people do have lives and are not always available to chat.

There are other strategies that you can make use of to help ease your

concerns when you are having a rough time.

Continue with the next few chapters to uncover them.

CHAPTER 6

HAVE A NAP

You would not believe how much this has helped me in the past, when I first cleaned up and even to this day.

You could be having the worst day in the world, thinking your life is terrible and the only thing that will help numb the pain is getting fucked up.

Just make the conscious decision to go home, get undressed, go under your blankets and go to sleep so you can wake up and start over fresh.

It's a fact that when most of us think we are having a bad day, we are really just having a bad moment within a day.

Each day is just made up of hundreds of short little moments.

Maybe you had 5 bad moments today, which yes, is making your day seem terrible.

You can always start over and make your next moment better.

Maybe your last 5 moments are still too fresh in your mind and you cant keep thinking about them.

This is when you should look at the rest of the day and see if you can find something to look forward to.

If you don't have anything going on later, create something where you work on yourself or help someone else.

Have a nap, wake up, have a shower and re-start the day so that it is now an awesome day.

Don't accept anything less.

CHAPTER 7

FOOD

Spicy food in particular works the best for me.

It literally has saved me from the strongest cravings many times.

Sometimes, you are just not in a position to nap but you still need something to clear your mind.

Nothing makes you stop thinking about something more than your mouth burning off of you because of some hot chilis in your Pho (Vietnamese soup.)

.

I remember the first time that this saved me.

I was about 3 days clean and went out to an event which was put on by my meeting fellowship.

I was having a pretty good time with my new friends but one girl (who was drop dead gorgeous) told me that her friends are having a big biker music festival out of town and suggested that we should go and set up a tent and do it sober.

Instantly I started thinking about everything that could go wrong.

Part of me however, was trying to rationalize it telling me that maybe we could go and stay sober and have a good time.

It sounded like my ideal kind of party.

Music festival, camping, girls, dancing, fun times right?

Deep down though, I knew that it would be trouble.

I even agreed to go with her later and said it would be fun.

Luckily my extreme anxiety kicked in and I left to go home and switch my laundry and never went back.

I was panicking after that.

Its crazy how it literally only takes one sentence and you can go from committed to your decision on staying clean to putting yourself out there in a very dangerous situation where you would almost certainly be putting your sobriety (and life) at risk.

I remember pulling over my car and trying to call and text my
supports for the first time.

Nobody would answer and I immediately felt like everybody hated
me and wanted me to fail.

I was just dying for a shot of whisky or a giant line of anything.

I really just wanted a kick in the face.

I don't know what made me think of it, but I decided instead to get
that kick to the face in the form of some really spicy food.

As I had no money, I could only afford to get a bottle of hot sauce and brought it home and made some super spicy pasta with meatballs.

After I finished eating, my mouth was burning so bad the last thing I was thinking about was getting high.

It basically reset my day without a nap by taking my mind off of whatever was bugging me before.

Eventually my supports called me back and I explained my issue and how I solved it.

They were very proud of me and came by for some pasta.

CHAPTER 8

TAKE ACTION

Do what you have to do.

Whatever your plan was make the action to carry it out.

Whether it is going to a meeting, making a phone call, sending a text, or just admitting to yourself that you have a problem, take action.

A plan without action is just a thought and will get you nowhere.

Maybe your first attempt will fail, but keep trying until you get it.

If and when you do fail, REVISE your plan and try again.

This is crucial.

I am sure you have heard that "doing the same thing over and over and expecting different results is the definition of insanity."

Whoever did say it, was definitely right.

If something doesn't work, you have to make a change or the results will stay the same.

Unfortunately, sometimes it is impossible to realize this until it's too late.

I am no exception.

I can vividly remember deciding to quit drugs 4 different times.

Each time, I made a plan and took action on it.

Unfortunately for me, the first 3 times I proceeded with the same plan.

You may be able to relate.

Basically each time, I would decide to quit drugs.

In order to do this, I would basically seclude myself from everybody I know and stay in the house.

I would focus my time on something else like my school, work or the gym.

I was actually somewhat successful with this strategy in that I would go about 6 months each time, which is much longer than most people make it.

At the 6-month mark however, I would feel lonely or secluded from the world and would give in to the human need to be social.

In a momentary lapse, I would actually desire to communicate with other people.

Unfortunately the only way I knew how to meet people or socialize was by inviting them out for a drink.

A couple of times I even convinced myself I was able to go out for a drink and stop after that.

Once, it even worked like that for one occurrence.

I had one drink and went home. Everything seemed fine.

The next weekend however, I did the same thing but finished my

drink in literally 30 seconds and ordered a second one.

Halfway through the second one, I was on the phone ordering up

some cocaine and planning a summer of music festivals, ketamine,

ecstasy and hallucinogens.

It's funny how quickly you can go from clean and sober to neck deep

into a bender.

This type of addiction is beyond dangerous, it's lethal.

People are right to call it a disease.

Not only are you putting your life in danger but are putting other

peoples as well.

It's hard to make sense that so much harm can be done to so many

people if you just decided to have one drink.

I know nobody does drugs with a direct intensions on using it to

harm others but unfortunately that is what happens.

It will hurt the lives not only of yourself, your friends and family but

even the lives innocent people you have never met.

Addiction is one of the most powerful and destructive forces

imaginable and it is crucial that you do your best to control it before

it controls you.

This being said, the 4th and final time I quit, I realized I needed a new plan.

I remember being in a hotel room, standing on the balcony, looking down 20 floors to the black cement, calling everybody I knew, hoping someone would talk me off the edge.

I was flirting with the idea of ending my life because I felt that quitting drugs was impossible, only remembering every other time being hopeless and lonely with no one to turn to for comfort except the drugs.

Talking to people did take me off the ledge and back into the hotel room but did not let me feel any better or more confident for a new tomorrow.

It got me through the moment but I was still frustrated with needing a new plan so I could feel that life was in fact worth living.

I vividly remember coming to the realization that if I really was going to survive this, I needed to find other people who have went through it and survived long enough to come out the other side with healthy and happy social relationships free of drugs.

For a little while I was unsure if people like this really exist.

Then I remembered when I was a child and was caught drinking to the point where I had enough alcohol in my system to kill a 350 pound man, my father took me to a 12-step fellowship meeting for people with a problem with alcohol.

At the time, I did not feel like I could relate.

I thought of it more as a punishment than anything.

Picture me sitting there a young 15-year-old punk kid in a room full of old men talking about their alcohol problems.

At the time, it seemed pointless.

But now, all of these years later, I knew I was there for a reason.

It was because of this memory that 13 years later I thought of

searching on Google for fellowship meetings for people who are

addicted to drugs.

I found out that there was actually a large amount of these meetings

every day in the city where I was heading.

I spent the rest of the night doing the last of my drugs and debating the idea of flushing them (mostly because they stopped working anyways) while at the same time writing a speech that I thought I would have to give the next afternoon when I went to my first meeting. (Which by the way is not what they do.)

Seven hours later, I finally finished writing this speech. I proceeded to flush the rest of my drugs down the toilet and went to bed.

It was kind of easy at that point because the drugs stopped working about 3 days prior.

I had the tolerance of a horse.

I actually fell asleep pretty quickly, probably because I was crashing down after a 10-day, $12,000 bender of uppers, downers and all-arounders.

Let me again re-emphasize, you DO NOT have to let it get that far.

The next day I woke up and drove back to the city and straight to the location of my first meeting.

I remember pulling up right at 12:00pm when it was set to start.

It was at an addictions support building.

At that time, the word addict really just scared me away.

I immediately was second-guessing my choices on going there.

I was terrified.

I parked around the corner and walked up to the front door but couldn't bring myself to opening the door.

I seen people inside, got scared and then just kept walking around the block, back to my car and drove home to my bed where I hid for another day.

It was the day after when again I went back to the meeting, this time I went a half hour early.

It was a sunny August afternoon and there was a small group of people smoking out front.

Again, I parked around the corner and started walking towards the people in front.

I had no idea what I was going to do.

Could I even bring myself to talk to them?

I remember thinking "but they're drug addicts."

I didn't know if I was going to be stabbed or punched in the face.

I was absolutely terrified but kept walking towards the two guys standing out front.

I slowed down a bit when I got close to them and said hi.

All of a sudden they started talking to me.

These were some of the nicest people I have ever met.

I asked them if there is a meeting going on in there.

They enthusiastically said yes! Go on in. Grab a seat.

They genuinely seemed happy to see me.

When I got in there was about 15 chairs set up but only about 2

people sitting around.

I felt like everybody was looking at me but at second glance I realized

nobody was.

The 2 guys I met outside came in and helped organize the meeting

and make the coffee.

I noticed one of the guys had a keychain that supported the logo for

an electronic music promotion company I followed.

I instantly felt connected to these guys.

They were close to my age and I could see myself being friends with

them.

Then the guy at the front of the room started the meeting.

Hi my name is _ and I'm an addict.

A few more people slowly came into the meeting and took their seat.

They went through the program and how it works.

Different people took turns reading and sharing their own experiences.

I instantly knew that's where I needed to be.

I felt a strong connection and common bond with each person who spoke.

It was a "birthday meeting" for someone who was celebrating his first year clean.

Everybody was celebrating and saying nice things about how far this person has come.

It was amazing.

It was so hard for me to comprehend just how far I have come in just 24 hours.

From being all alone balancing on edge at the top of a hotel balcony, to feeling so grounded with strong connections to other individuals at a recovery meeting.

All through the meeting, I was waiting for my turn to speak.

I stayed up all night preparing and typing out what I was going to say.

I had it printed off and in my pocket.

I noticed nobody else has anything prepared and people just spoke from their heart while sitting at their seat.

This was very relieving.

Then, they asked if anybody was new to the program and would like to identify themselves by their first name.

I did and everybody said hi & welcome.

At the end of the meeting, they asked if anybody else would like to share.

I have been working myself up and might have just exploded if I didn't get a chance to share what I have been preparing all night and really my entire life.

I introduced myself and went onto blurt out much of what I had built up inside of me.

I let them know that it was my first day clean, I overdosed and died less than 72 hours before and was revived and brought myself to come to that meeting.

I let them know that I have had enough and do not want to die anymore.

Most importantly, I now realized that it is possible for people to go through what I went through and continued to move on, surviving and thriving.

Everybody clapped and they were so happy that I shared.

For the more experienced people in the meetings, it is important that they hear from people who are freshly clean.

It reminds them of what they escaped from and shows them that its not getting any better out there.

After I shared, they gave me a list with phone numbers for other people who are in the program and were happy to help me in my efforts to stay clean.

☐

CHAPTER 9

GET SUPPORT

At the end of that meeting, it was said that if you still need to share,

grab someone and go for a coffee.

Knowing that I really needed support to get through this and was

dying to meet some sober friends, I helped clean up a bit and asked

the guys who put the meeting on if they would go for a coffee.

They agreed and also gave me their phone numbers.

After cleaning up, everybody went out for a cigarette.

I felt as if I was given a new life.

I felt, as I was now part of this new family.

I now had a group of awesome new people who did not do drugs and were happy to help support me in what was to come.

Everybody seemed to know each other very well.

They were all laughing and getting along like best friends.

Some with 30 years clean and some just a few hours but everybody treated equal.

About 5 of us ended up going for coffee and they all expressed how

proud they were of me for sharing on my first day.

A lot of people are way too scared to their first day.

One lady gave me this old book that you could tell has been passed

down from addict to addict.

They all wrote notes inside and left me with their phone numbers.

This was the start of something great.

I now knew that I was not alone in this fight and I have people that I can reach out to who have been through the same things as me and have made it out.

One of the older guys at these meetings really reminded me of my father.

I remember sharing at a meeting about how my father went to meetings as well.

I expressed that I wanted to wait until I had 6 months clean before I tell my father that I am in the program.

After the meeting this older gentleman suggested that I probably didn't have to wait that long and he was right.

After about 2 weeks, I let my father and mother know that I started going to meetings.

At first, I could only tell them it was so I could quit drinking because I still could not bring myself to say out loud that I was a drug addict or even that I have done drugs.

They were very happy and relieved.

They actually became some of my strongest supports.

I would call them every day just to check in and talk about our days.

This helped keep me accountable as well as not feel so anti-social.

My sister was also a huge support because luckily she lived in the same city at this time and I literally hung out with her every evening during this period.

You really cannot get a support network quick enough.

Every minute left without support, is a minute you are chancing the possibility of tricking yourself into doing drugs again.

Literally in the blink of an eye, you can go from working on staying sober to knee deep into a bag of blow.

CHAPTER 10

FILL YOUR TIME WITH POSITIVITY

Idle time is the devils playground.

You really need to find something to do with all of your time.

Luckily, I still had a job that took up most of my time and mental ability.

I was trapped out at an oil camp for 21 days at a time.

It's not to say there weren't drugs around at work but I was lucky enough to be in a position where nobody would ever tell me who had them anyways.

Being clean during this time was easy for me because I never got into that habit of using while I was at work.

Plus, I was just too busy working 18 hours per day.

It was the 7 days off that I had a problem with.

Striving to stay clean, and with my team of supports, I have

learned to fill these 7 days with positivity.

Basically, I would start every day with a meeting.

Call my parents in the afternoon, then have dinner and hang out

with my sister in the evening.

If there was one thing I desired it was a routine with no idle time

where I would get inside my head.

Some of the things we would do in the evening would be like to go to an arcade, Chuckie Cheese, the movies, bowling and sometimes just stay in and watch TV.

One thing that was a given however, is food.

I would make us some awesome meals.

It's funny how you forget about the little things like that when you are using.

Another thing I would do every afternoon while I waited for my sister to finish work was going to the gym and pool I had in my apartment building.

The funny thing was that we chose that apartment building because it had a pool but none of us have ever went to it, until I cleaned up.

You would be amazed how many super fun things are actually available in life once you let go of your distractions and go out looking for them.

Every day there was something awesome happening, which I would have missed out on if I were still using.

I learned to just sit back and enjoy the sunshine and other blessings such as my family, new friends and other people in the program.

One day, my friend asked me and another new guy in the program, if we would like to go to a movie after the meeting.

I haven't gone to a movie in about 10 years.

I went and it was the best time ever.

Another day, we all went and watched football at someone's

house.

I was never a sports fan but loved having something new to do

and fill my time with positivity.

The next week, they all came over to my house for football.

It was great entertaining sober people.

Enjoyed snacks, laughing and had a great time.

It was nice to enjoy life without all of the hurt, shame and wasted

time and money from my time in active addiction.

It really was day and night, the difference from when I was using

to when I finally stopped and learned to enjoy life, clean and sober.

CHAPTER 11

STAY AWAY FROM RELATIONSHIPS

This cannot be stressed enough.

You might think during this time more than ever, you will need that relationship.

A shoulder to cry on is always nice and when you are going through a time in your life when you are always crying.

It can be crucial, but find it elsewhere.

Your family, parents, brother, sister, people in your support group, hell even a Walmart greeter, but whatever you do, do not enter into a romantic relationship (or make any major life decisions) for your first year clean.

You will want to, probably more than anything but it will surely

lead to your demise.

So many people do not listen to this suggestion and when that

relationship does not work out or even when you get into a fight

down the road over something stupid, you will end up using.

So, don't do it.

Short-term gains are not worth the long-term pains.

If you are in a poison relationship, end it.

Run away!

It worked for me, for a bit anyways.

Don't go back like I did months later only to piss away 2 years of recovery and pretty much start over mentally.

Quitting a relationship is a lot like quitting drugs.

Do these same suggestions.

Make a plan, stick to it and temporarily replace your time with something else to get through the rough parts.

As addicts, we are very obsessive.

We would jump in the habit of quitting one thing and moving on

to another.

So many times I would quit one drug and then find myself a week

later gripping on to a new one.

This is a very dangerous trait that we have, but if done right, we can use it to our advantage.

Now, I don't mean quit heroin and move down to blow, or alcohol, weed or even coffee.

I mean try and move your addiction onto a recovery program or reading or best-of-all balance.

I am at a point in my recovery now, where I am striving to be more balanced.

Making myself more organized and scheduled and overall more mentally stable.

If you can figure out to strive for this early, you will be well on your way.

CHAPTER 12

CHANGE YOUR PLAN

When things go wrong, which they will, know that you can always make a change.

Maybe you don't listen to the last step like so many of us and you decide to enter into a relationship because your lonely or you think you are cured from your addiction. Then you find out your loved one is using or they convince you that you can have one beer on Christmas only to the next week spiral out of control into a bender from New Years to Valentines day.

Being still new at quitting drugs, you are kicking one excessively obsessive substance, if you move that obsession over to another person, when that person doesn't work out, you feel like you need something else to move that obsession to and chances are you will turn back to drugs.

Instead, recognize your addiction early and work at keeping it in check by listening to these suggestions and getting off drugs for once and for all.

What happens when your plan fails, or you fuck things up and fall away from the plan?

You change your plan or make the decision to start following it again.

You need to take a look at why the plan failed or why you fucked it up and make a decision to modify your thinking or behaviors so that you will not be put in that same position.

You might have to change your plan every day but as long as you continue in the right direction, you will get there.

You are entering into a new life where you are constantly learning and changing is key to your success in overcoming this demon.

CHAPTER 13

LEARN MORE

All around us are lessons that we can learn from.

Make the decision to start learning from those lessons.

Learn about yourself, what sets you off, what makes you happy, what makes you feel good.

Maybe connecting with other people makes you feel good.

If so, then make an effort to connect with new people.

Maybe you find that going to a certain part of the city sets you off, stay the fuck out of that part of the city.

Another option would be to go back to school or take some

online courses.

While these options are definitely a good use of time and can help

to get you through the short term initial phases of trying to get clean,

I wouldn't go making them the sole part of your strategy to

staying clean because much like switching to a less harmful substance,

their effects are only temporary.

Now, if you can make learning one strategy in a well-balanced overall plan, it can be key to your spiritual and mental growth.

Learning about yourself and the world around you can be key to kicking the nasty bug of addiction.

Maybe you were an aggressive person in the past.

Maybe through learning about yourself, you realize that you are aggressive because you are actually hurt inside, which has made you aggressive.

The faster you face your own problems head on, the faster you will be able to move on and grow into a better person.

Going forward, maybe you will realize that when someone is being aggressive or negative towards you, you will understand that they are just dealing with some personal issues and it really has nothing to do with you and you can just move on and continue with your day.

CHAPTER 14

LOVE MORE

Deep down we are all just stuck, longing for unconditional love.

Give yourself that love.

Learn to love yourself.

If you cannot figure out what to love about yourself, start doing something different.

Help someone out.

Even if you have nothing to share, you have your time.

Volunteer somewhere.

Help out at a homeless shelter.

Go to an animal shelter; ask to volunteer playing with the animals.

When I first got clean, after a meeting, someone told me that they are going to go and pet cats at an animal shelter.

If you don't feel more love, playing in a room of kittens, you probably are not human.

If animals aren't your thing, go to a seniors home and ask for

volunteer opportunities.

They would love to have some young blood in the door to share

their time with.

Go plant a garden.

Make art and donate it.

Search online for volunteer opportunities in your area.

If there aren't any, create some.

Time really is your most valuable asset.

You can always make more money, you can always get more things, but you will never be able to get more time.

To share it with somebody else really is the most generous thing you could do.

CHAPTER 15

BE HONEST

As addicts, we have spent years lying, cheating and stealing.

This will make it an extremely hard trait to break but definitely something to work towards.

The most important thing is to stop lying to yourself.

We tend to be very smart and manipulative when dealing with other people, but this power is exponentially stronger when lying to ourselves.

Try to recognize when you are lying and be brutally honest with yourself and some trusted friends.

This is another reason why I like meetings because you can be brutally honest and nobody there will judge you.

Even if they do, who gives a fuck?

You are there to heal and as long as you are healing that is all that matters.

If you get a feeling that one person is judging you, I can guarantee 10 other people in the same room madly respect you.

Learn and grow to be more and more honest every day.

You might not have as many friends, but you will have the right ones.

It is much better to have 1 true friend than 1000 fake ones.

CHAPTER 16

KEEP AN OPEN MIND

Be open to what the world has to offer.

There are great opportunities out there and you can do anything with your life if you try.

You will meet some people with great knowledge so keep an open mind and absorb the greatness.

These people have already went through what you are going through and came out the other side much better at life and feeling good.

You will hear some ideas that sound absolutely insane and sure some of them might be, but don't jump to that conclusion right away.

If someone says that you should write down things you are grateful for or say the serenity prayer each morning maybe it could help you where you are.

Maybe someone could tell you to start praying but you are strongly against religion.

Maybe you should do it anyways; if for no other reason but just to reflect on your day and see what areas you can try and focus on going forward.

Maybe they say to get phone numbers and actually pick up the phone and call them.

Going to 90 meetings in 90 days is another suggestion I hear a lot.

People either tend to think that's insane and avoid it or they double it and do 2 per day.

They are all great suggestions and if your mind is open, you would have great success with your recovery.

Some of these ideas might sound ludacris at the start but there are some suggestions that could honestly save your life.

It could be important to listen to them and you will not listen if your mind is closed off to anything that you do not agree with right away.

CHAPTER 17

CREATE SOMETHING

Whether its art, business, new friendships or a construction project, create something awesome.

You have probably spent years tearing these types of things apart so its your time to start creating or at very least helping make something better.

Use all of your extra time to work on a side project.

You have spent an enormous amount of time and money on finding, getting, using and dealing with the aftermath of drugs, focus these resources on something else.

Start a new course.

Create knowledge.

Create happiness in yourself or someone else.

It doesn't even have to be somebody you know.

Create joy.

Write a book.

Do a puzzle.

Paint a picture.

Use your time for something good, no, great.

Create something amazing!

Even if its not amazing, you will be glad you did it!

CHAPTER 18

FIND A HIGHER POWER

This one seems to take most people some time; I know it did for me.

If you go to any of the 12 step meeting fellowships, many if not all of them speak of a need for belief in a higher power.

It doesn't matter what your higher power is or whether you are religious or not, just know that there is something out there greater than you.

This is a hard thing to accept for most addicts.

Being an addict, we like to think that we are in control and we are the best and smartest at everything.

We know it all right?

I know I did.

Or so I thought.

That's why the belief in a higher power seemed so ridiculous when I first cleaned up but I took some advice that was once given to me.

Fake it until you make it.

Just go through the motions and admit your faults to a higher

power.

You can do this by praying.

Saying it out loud also does something immensely powerful to

your life.

You can also write it down.

Writing is a super powerful way to get things out and off your

chest.

Maybe writing this book is even helping me get a few things

straight in my mind.

Don't worry if you are not feeling this suggestion as of yet, but the quicker you can turn your will over to a loving and supporting god, the quicker you can stop worrying about what will go wrong and start getting excited about what is going right.

I cant remember the exact moment I started to believe but I remember a lot of little moments where it all made sense.

One of them was when I hit one year clean and I flew my father across the country to come and celebrate it with me.

When travelling around the Rocky Mountains, we were both amazed by the beauty of the mountains.

He asked me about my thoughts on this concept of a higher power and I was still unsure.

Growing up, he never came to church with us so I never thought of him as being very religious.

As we were driving however, he let me know about his beliefs.

He said that he is not sure what is out there but there is a very slim likelihood that everything just happened randomly.

All the mountains were placed here perfectly for the wildlife and the air is all made perfectly for life to be develop and thrive into what it is today.

For all of the planets in the sky, we really must be insanely lucky to be placed in the spec where we are located.

I never really noticed it like that.

Maybe I am a little naïve to think that maybe the mountains are just a giant piece of rock and people created roads to get places.

Breathable air, while being super highly unlikely, might just make us super, super incredibly lucky to be living here.

I noticed my higher power however to be true through my own experiences.

I notice it a lot when I go to meetings or see my supports.

Whenever I am having a rough time and then I reach out, I always hear exactly what I need to in order to get out of the rut I am feeling.

When I most noticed it however is when I think about all of the things which have led to me to where I am today.

□

When I overdosed and died, that could have easily been the end

for me.

I was out cold on the ground and not breathing.

There are a number of things which have led me

to live.

The first of all was everybody else I was with also died on that

ground .

That might not sound like a blessing, but if it was just myself,

maybe nobody would have got us help.

But people did go to get help.

Not the first person, as he was just trying to hide the bodies,

but our neighbors seen us and immediately started running to get

help.

Next was the medical professionals and security who came,

got us on the golf carts and brought us to safety.

☐

Also, just being at the right party which had these medical

professionals trained and prepared for this situation.

I have been to hundreds of parties where I could have died but it
was at this exact one where I finally did.

The fact that I woke up,

hoses coming from my veins,

medical professionals all around,

pumping adrenalin mixed blood to counteract the drug cocktail

running through my body.

The fact that it worked and I woke up

unlike so many people before me.

Brought back to life to see my friends still unconscious laying next to me surrounded with doctors trying to jumpstart their blood streams.

The fact that my disease of addiction sent me back out the very next day as soon as I found new drugs to play.

The fact that 2 days later, I hated all of my friends for 2 more days decided to keep partying, but did it all alone.

The fact that I got super depressed.
Barely made it to the city wanting to die, trying to die.

The fact that something popped in my head and told me there is a way out.

☐

The fact that I in my state of panic, I decided to Google addiction

meeting groups and found one the next day in the city where I was

heading.

The fact that I walked into that meeting and instantly connected

with 3 people who were just like me.

The fact that since then

I have learned that a sober life is not only possible,

but fucking amazing.

The fact that I now help other people to escape the life of active

addiction on a daily basis.

The fact that I can now write these types of books and create

different media to help others on a larger scale.

The fact that you are now reading this.

All these types of facts are the reasons why I truly understand with

all of my heart that there is a higher power and they want me to live

on to tell my story and listen to yours.

CHAPTER 19

DON'T GIVE UP

This is hands down the most important thing.

Whatever you do, don't give up.

Just keep moving forward.

It doesn't matter how slow you go or how long it takes you to "get it," in fact most people never actually "get it" and when you think you do, you will almost certainly prove yourself wrong.

Don't give up on recovery.

Don't give up on life.

Don't give up on yourself.

You are worth your spot on this earth, even if you don't see it

right now.

When everything seems like it's going to shit, you can make a

change.

If you can't figure out what change to make, reach out.

Contact someone.

If you don't know who to contact, Google it.

There is support out there.

Find a meeting.

Hell, send me an email or give me a call.

Look up Festival Addict. Send me a DM or Email.

Let me be your support.

I am here for you.

I can help point you in the right direction.

When you are having a shitty day, start over.

Have a nap, eat some super fucking spicy food.

It will give you the kick in the face that you are looking for.

Go for a run. Hit the gym.

Whatever you have to do, you can do it.

I believe in you.

CHAPTER 20

TAKE ACTION

What are you doing still here?

Go!

Get out there!

Get your notebook!

Look up a meeting!

Go through the suggestions, make your plan, get your supports

and work your program!

You can do it.

You are worth it.

Many people, myself included have been where you are right now and have got out of it and went on to live happy lives.

Those struggling addicts who do not seek recovery ALWAYS end up with the same results: jails, institutions and death.

Maybe you have experience with some of those results already but I just want you to know, that doesn't have to be the end for you.

You do not have to go that route.

Find someone who has went through it and came out the other

side a better person.

Find out what worked for them and what didn't.

Take their suggestions and listen to them.

Like I said, if you cant find a meeting or group or you have no

supports or nobody to talk to, look me up and I'll help you out.

Even if you just want to say hi, look me up.

I look forward to hearing from you.

Now get out there and be great!

I believe in you.

ABOUT THE AUTHOR

Obsessed with the creation of value, Stanley Arthur has always been an entrepreneur at heart. Ever since a young child, he has been a hustler and was driven to create something out of nothing. Starting with buying and selling video games at just 4 years old, he moved his way up to bicycles and eventually to drugs. Drugs lead him to the life of a DJ and after a 13 year struggle with addiction, Stanley overdosed and died. Having been brought back to life, he made the decision to devote his life to helping others. Still with the creation of value but instead focusing on the value held within our souls, "Stan 2.0" now devotes his life to spreading joy and awareness to addicts all over the world with his Festival Addict movement. Keep your eyes peeled for the upcoming trilogy of novels under the Festival Addict name which is loosely based on Stanley's life. Keep an eye out for Festival Addict online and stay tuned for much more to come.

Peace – Love – Unity – Respect

-Festival Addict

www.festivaladdict.me

Made in the USA
Columbia, SC
01 May 2017